S0-ALN-830

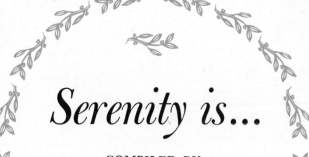

Serenity is...

COMPILED BY
GILBERT HAY

AN ESSANDESS® SPECIAL EDITION
New York

SERENITY IS . . .
S.B.N.: 671-10348-2
Copyright © 1969 by Gilbert Hay, S.T.
Published by Essandess Special Editions,
a division of Simon & Schuster, Inc.,
630 Fifth Avenue, New York, N.Y. 10020,
and on the same day in Canada
by Simon & Schuster of Canada, Ltd.,
Richmond Hill, Ontario.
Printed in the U.S.A.

ACKNOWLEDGMENTS

For arrangements made with various authors and publishing houses where copyrighted material was permitted to be reprinted and for the courtesy extended by them, the following acknowledgments are gratefully made. All possible care has been taken to trace the ownership of every selection included and to make full acknowledgment for its use. If any errors have accidentally occurred, they will be corrected in subsequent editions, provided notification is sent to the publisher.

Abingdon Press, for permission to use material by May Detherage and Arthur Helps from *Sunrise to Starlight*, compiled by May Detherage, copyright © 1966 by Abingdon Press.

Rupert Crew Limited, for permission to use material by Faith Forsyte from *The Encyclopedia of Religious Quotations*.

Sidney Greenberg, for permission to use material by Frances Shaw from *Treasury of the Art of Living*, edited by Sidney Greenberg, copyright © 1963 by Hartmore House, Hartford.

The Estate of Rufus M. Jones, for permission to use material from "The Testimony of The Soul" from *The World Treasury of Religious Quotations*.

Newsweek Magazine, for permission to use material by Dr. Carl Jung from an article in the August 1, 1960 issue.

Dr. Reinhold Niebuhr, for permission to use material from "The Irony of American History" from *The World Treasury of Religious Quotations*.

Pyramid Publications, Inc., for permission to use material by Elaine Budd from "Beauty Today" from *Young in Heart*.

Charles Scribner's Sons for permission to use material by Henry Van Dyke from *Live Your Life*, edited by W. F. Heiby, published by Harper & Row.

Gladys Taber, for permission to use her material.

Dr. Charles L. Wallis, for permission to use material by George Santayana, Mary McLeod Bethune, William S. Ogden, Richard E. Byrd and Ida Norton Munson from *Words of Life*, edited by Charles L. Wallis, copyright © 1966.

Wesleyan University Press, for permission to use material by W. H. Davies from "Light from Many Lamps" from *The Complete Poems of W. H. Davies*, copyright © 1963 by Jonathan Cape Limited.

For
Bea *and* Dinty

To read, to think,
to love, to hope, to pray:
these are the things
that make for serenity.

JOHN RUSKIN

Serenity of heart is his
who cares for neither praise nor blame.

THOMAS À KEMPIS

A man's moments of serenity may be few,
but a few will sustain him a lifetime.

RICHARD E. BYRD

An old man surprised everyone with his cheerfulness, since he seemed to have an unusual amount of trouble and relatively few pleasures. When asked the secret of his cheery disposition, he replied: "Well, you see, it's like this. The Bible says often, 'And it came to pass,' never, 'It came to stay.'"

For the man sound in body
and serene of mind
there is no such thing as bad weather.

GEORGE GISSING

If seeds in the black earth
can turn into such beautiful roses,
what might not the heart of man become
in its long journey to God?

Peace, like every other
rare and precious thing,
doesn't come to you.
You have to go and get it.

FAITH FORSYTE

It is the nature of a great mind
to be calm and undisturbed.

SENECA

The beginning of wisdom
is the realization that
the thing you are anxious about today
won't seem important tomorrow.

Those who see the beauty
of a flaming sunset
do not fear the night.
There will be the splendor
of a million stars!

Take therefore no thought for the morrow;
for the morrow shall take thought
for the things of itself.

MATTHEW 6:34

No one is happy unless he is
reasonably well satisfied with himself,
so that the quest for serenity
must of necessity begin
with self-examination.

WILLIAM S. OGDEN

Seek not that everything
should happen as you wish,
but wish for everything
to happen as it does,
and you will be serene.

EPICTETUS

The secret of a happy and serene life
is to be content with
the abilities God gave you.

How restful are unhurried things!
  The spreading light of dawn's gray hour,
Slow, rhythmic motion of birds' wings,
  The opening petals of a flower.

Dim shadows moving on a wall,
  The moon's calm light above the bay,
Soft murmurings that rise and fall
  Within the dusk that hushes day.

My journey, too, may bring content
    To the still place of heart's desire;
There, tranquilly, to pitch my tent,
    Watch flames scale heavenward
            from my fire.

IDA NORTON MUNSON

To me every hour of the light and dark
is a miracle,
Every cubic inch of space is a miracle.

WALT WHITMAN

Nor hell nor heaven shall that soul
surprise,
Who loves the rain,
And loves his home,
And looks on life with quiet eyes.

FRANCES SHAW

It is only in contemplative moments
that life is truly vital.

GEORGE SANTAYANA

In quietness and in trust shall be
your strength.

ISAIAH 30:15

Serenity exists where there is,
in addition to the things that
bring satisfaction and contentment,
a conscious awareness that one has
these things. Most of us have the
first qualification for happiness:
we have an abundance of blessings.
It is in the second area that we
fall short: we fail to recognize
the fact that we have all these things.

With a few flowers in my garden,
half a dozen pictures and some books,
I live without envy.

LOPE DE VEGA

All I see teaches me
to trust the Creator
for all I do not see.

No one is born completely cheerful
or completely irritable.
A serene disposition we acquire,
then develop through practice
and more practice.

EILEEN CADE-EDWARDS

The best things are the nearest:
breath in your nostrils,
light in your eyes,
flowers at your feet,
duties at your hand,
the path of Right just before you.
Do not grasp at the stars,
but do life's plain, common work
as it comes,
certain that daily duties and daily bread
are the sweetest things of life.

ROBERT LOUIS STEVENSON

Give me, kind heaven, a private station,
a mind serene for contemplation.

JOHN GAY

No man ever injured his eyesight
by looking
on the bright side of things.

An inability to stay quiet
is one of the most conspicuous
failings of mankind.

WALTER BAGEHOT

If one sets aside time for a business appointment, a trip to the hairdresser, a social engagement, or a shopping expedition, that time is accepted as inviolable. But if one says: I cannot come because that is my hour to be alone, one is considered rude, egotistical or strange. What a commentary on our civilization, when being alone is considered suspect; when one has to apologize for it, make excuses, hide the fact that one practices it—like a secret vice!

Actually these are among the most important times in one's life— when one is alone. Certain springs are tapped only when we are alone.

ANNE MORROW LINDBERGH

The blue of heaven
is larger than the clouds.

ELIZABETH BARRETT BROWNING

Enjoy as many of your daily tasks
as you can.
Do the others
and enjoy having them behind you.

There are as many nights as days, and the one is just as long as the other in the year's course. Even a happy life cannot be without a measure of darkness, and the word "happy" would lose its meaning if it were not balanced by sadness. It is far better to take things as they come along with patience and equanimity.

DR. CARL JUNG

Reflect upon your blessings,
of which every man has many;
not on your misfortunes,
of which all men have some.

CHARLES DICKENS

Life, after all,
contains only one great problem:
That of so adjusting yourself
to the inevitable
so that you can remain calm and serene.
The greatest victory of life
is the conquest of worry.
The greatest discovery a man can make
is how to escape envy and hate.

DOUGLAS FREEMAN

All men's miseries derive from
not being able to sit quiet
in a room alone.

BLAISE PASCAL

God drops His anchor
only into the calm soul.

Serenity comes not alone by removing
the outward causes and occasions of fear,
but by the discovery
of inward reservoirs to draw upon.

RUFUS M. JONES

The best medicine for you to take
is yourself—
with a grain of salt.

Night, like a black velvet curtain
draped over the noises of the day;
like the quietness that comes
after a storm; like the coolness
to a fevered brow, comes Night.

Man, fulfilled with all he has taken of
life from Dawn until Night, serenely
folds his robes about him and releases
his responsibilities. The Morning Star
will shine again, but Man will greet
the new day in eternity.

MAY DETHERAGE

It is neither wealth nor splendor,
but serenity and occupation,
which give happiness.

THOMAS JEFFERSON

He who has little and wants less
is richer than he who has much
and wants more.

Every morning compose your soul for a tranquil day, and all through it be careful often to recall your resolution, and bring yourself back to it, so to say. If something discomposes you, do not be upset or troubled; but having discovered the fact, humble yourself gently before God, and try to bring your mind into a quiet attitude. Say to yourself: "Well, I have made a false step; now I must go more carefully and watchfully." Do this each time, however frequently you fall. When you are at peace use it profitably, making constant acts of meekness and seeking to be calm even in the most trifling things. Above all, do not be discouraged; be patient; wait; strive to attain a calm, gentle spirit.

ST. FRANCIS DE SALES

Because you have
occasional low spells of despondence,
don't despair.
The sun has a sinking spell
every night,
but it rises again all right
the next morning.

HENRY VAN DYKE

I *have learned,
in whatsoever state I am,
therewith to be content.*

PHILIPPIANS 4:11

I*f all our troubles were hung on a line,
    You would take yours
And I would take mine.*

Drink slowly, sip life's varied draught,
   And taste it as you go;
The sweetest vintage ever quaffed
   The hasty never know.

Be patient enough to live
one day at a time, as Christ taught us,
letting yesterday go,
and leaving tomorrow until it arrives.

Good humor is a tonic for mind
and body.
It is the best antidote for anxiety
and depression.
Is is the direct route to serenity
and contentment.

A few wise friends
with whom to counsel,
a few good books
to read and absorb, and,
with courage and faith,
we are well equipped
for the facing of life's
difficulties and disappointments,
as well as its pleasures
and successes.

PHILLIPS BROOKS

The most serene person is the one
who lives honestly, does his best,
lives one day at a time,
and refuses to worry.

What is this life if, full of care,
  We have no time to stand and stare.

No time to stand beneath the boughs
  And stare as long as sheep or cows.

No time to see, when woods we pass,
  Where squirrels hide their nuts in grass.

No time to see in broad daylight,
  Streams full of stars, like skies at night.

No time to turn at Beauty's glance,
  And watch her feet, how they can dance.

No time to wait till her mouth can
   Enrich that smile her eyes began.

A poor life this if, full of care,
   We have no time to stand and stare.

W. H. DAVIES

Resolve to be thyself; and know, that he
Who finds himself, loses his misery.

MATTHEW ARNOLD

If you would know
the greatest sum in addition,
count your blessings!

It is difficult to make a man miserable
while he feels he is worthy of himself
and claims kindred
to the great God who made him.

ABRAHAM LINCOLN

We can find great value in the phrase, "In God's good time." It helps us to learn to wait for the right solution of our problems. Patience depends on faith. When we have faith, we have inner peace which helps us face the future with serenity and without fear.

If wrinkles must be written
on our brows,
let them not be written
on the heart.
The spirit should not grow old.

JAMES A. GARFIELD

Quiet minds cannot be perplexed
or frightened,
but go on in fortune or misfortune
at their own private pace,
like a clock in a thunderstorm.

ROBERT LOUIS STEVENSON

Patience and the passage of time
solve all problems, cure all troubles,
dissipate all worries.

The best things in life move slowly.
They can hardly overtake one who is
in a hurry. We are making haste to
ill purpose if we "haven't time" to
read good books, to think quietly,
to visit our friends, to comfort
the sick and sorrowing, to enjoy the
beautiful creations of God and man, and
to lend a hand to a struggling brother.
Time is precious, but more precious
than fleeting hours are truth, love,
benevolence, friendship, service, a
serene mind, and a happy heart, for
these are the essence of life itself.

For age is opportunity no less
   Than youth itself, though in
      another dress,
And as the evening twilight fades away
   The sky is filled with stars
      invisible by day.

HENRY WADSWORTH LONGFELLOW

He is wise
who has endured all the pains of mankind
and still smiles serenely.

I *know the secret of peaceful living.*
I am not waiting for peace and happiness
to come to me in another world;
I am enjoying it here day by day.
Because of this growing, giving, learning
experience, I believe that I shall have
greater capacity for receiving when I
shall see Him who is the foundation of
my life.

MARY MCLEOD BETHUNE

To be seventy years young
is sometimes far more cheerful and
hopeful than to be forty years old.

OLIVER WENDELL HOLMES

The pleasures of the senses pass quickly:
those of the heart become sorrows;
but those of the mind are with us
to the end of our journey.

The final wisdom of life requires not the annulment of incongruity but the achievement of serenity within and above it.

REINHOLD NIEBUHR

Americans feel so guilty about taking
a rest . . . Nevertheless, everyone
needs a change of pace or a siesta.
Whatever became of the gentle art of
doing nothing at all?
Of lying in the grass
enjoying Spring sunshine,
or reading in a hammock,
or just sitting listening to music
on the radio or record player?

ELAINE BUDD

He who is of a calm and happy nature will hardly feel the pressure of age, but to him who is of an opposite disposition youth and age are equally a burden.

PLATO

We all seek happiness so eagerly,
that in the pursuit we often lose
that joyous sense of existence, and
those quiet daily pleasures, the values
of which our pride alone prevents us
from acknowledging.

It has been said with some meaning,
that if men would but rest in silence,
they might always hear the music
of the spheres.

ARTHUR HELPS

Waste no tears
upon the blotted record of lost years,
but turn the page and smile
to see the fair white pages that remain.

A secret of serenity
is not to do what you like,
but to like what you do.

A *time of quietude*
brings things into proportion
and gives us strength.
We all need to take time
from the busyness of living,
even if it be only ten minutes
to watch the sun go down
or the city lights
blossom against a canyoned sky.
We need time to dream,
time to remember,
and time to reach toward the infinite.
Time to be.

GLADYS TABER